While My Guitar Gently Sleeps

Jason Lee Christopher

While My Guitar Gently Sleeps
Copyright © 2020 by Jason Lee Christopher

All rights reserved. No part of this publication may be reproduced, distributed, or transmitted in any form or by any means, including photocopying, recording, or other electronic or mechanical methods, without the prior written permission of the author, except in the case of brief quotations embodied in critical reviews and certain other non-commercial uses permitted by copyright law.

Tellwell Talent
www.tellwell.ca

ISBN
978-0-2288-4401-3 (Hardcover)
978-0-2288-4400-6 (Paperback)
978-0-2288-4402-0 (eBook)

To Sloane and Emmett: I hope the love of music stays with you forever.

Please visit *jlcstorybooks.com* to download the audio lullaby of "While My Guitar Gently Sleeps."

While my guitar gently sleeps.

But the night is upon us; the day has grown long.

When tomorrow arrives, we'll strum together again,

Playing our songs from beginning to end.

While my guitar gently sleeps.

By:
Jason Lee Christopher